Apatosaurus (Brontosaurus)!
Fun Facts about the Apatosaurus
Dinosaurs for Children and Kids Edition

Children's Biological Science of Dinosaurs Books

PRODIGYWIZARD
BOOKS

Welcome to the world of Apatosaurus (Brontosaurus Dinosaurs)!

Let's learn where it lived, what it ate, how it performed and how big they were!

Check out and feel cool of these facts!

Apatosaurus also known as Brontosaurus is one of the giant dinosaurs ever roamed Earth. It could grow up to 23m or 75ft in length.

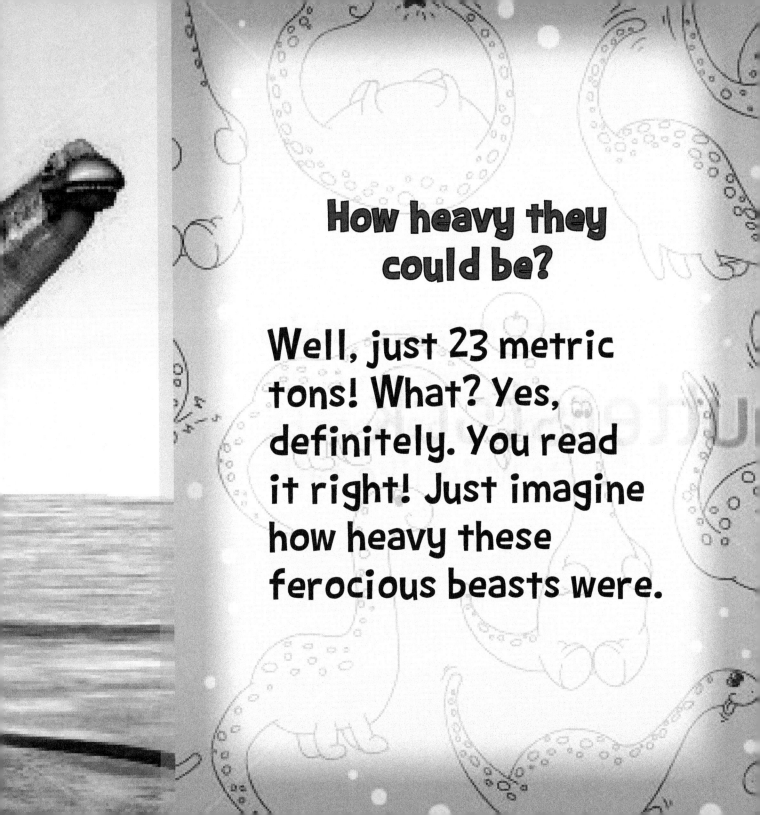

How heavy they could be?

Well, just 23 metric tons! What? Yes, definitely. You read it right! Just imagine how heavy these ferocious beasts were.

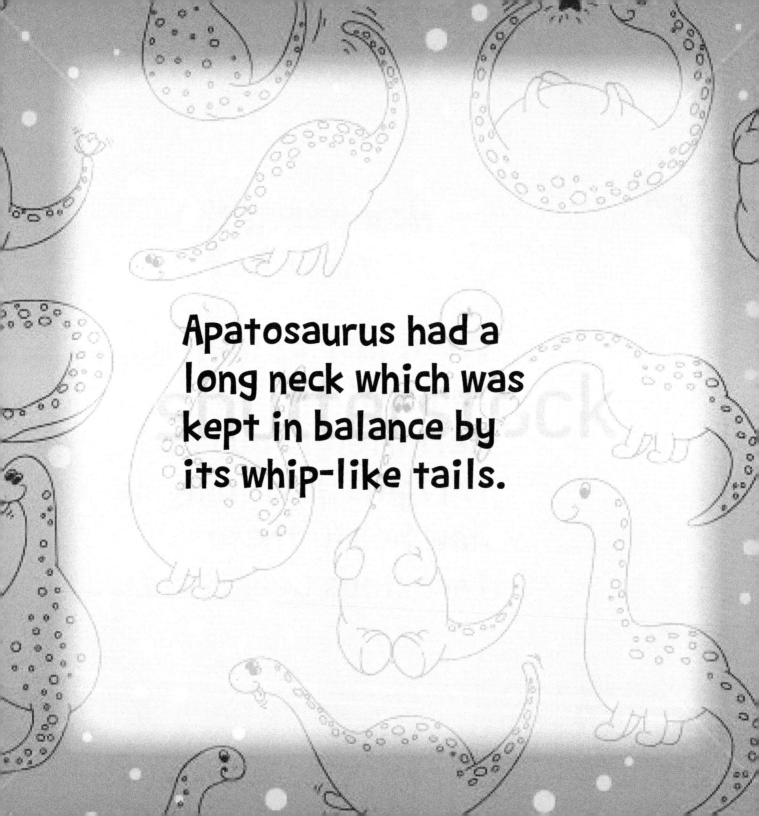

Apatosaurus had a long neck which was kept in balance by its whip-like tails.

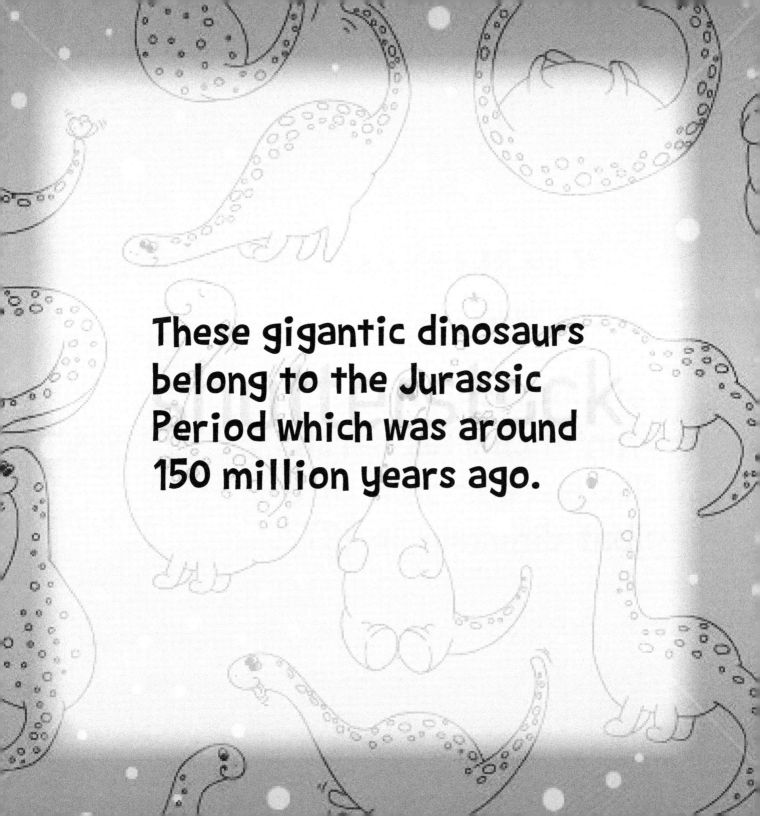

These gigantic dinosaurs belong to the Jurassic Period which was around 150 million years ago.

How did it get its two names?

Paleontologist Othniel Charles Marsh discovered bones of a giant dinosaur in 1877.

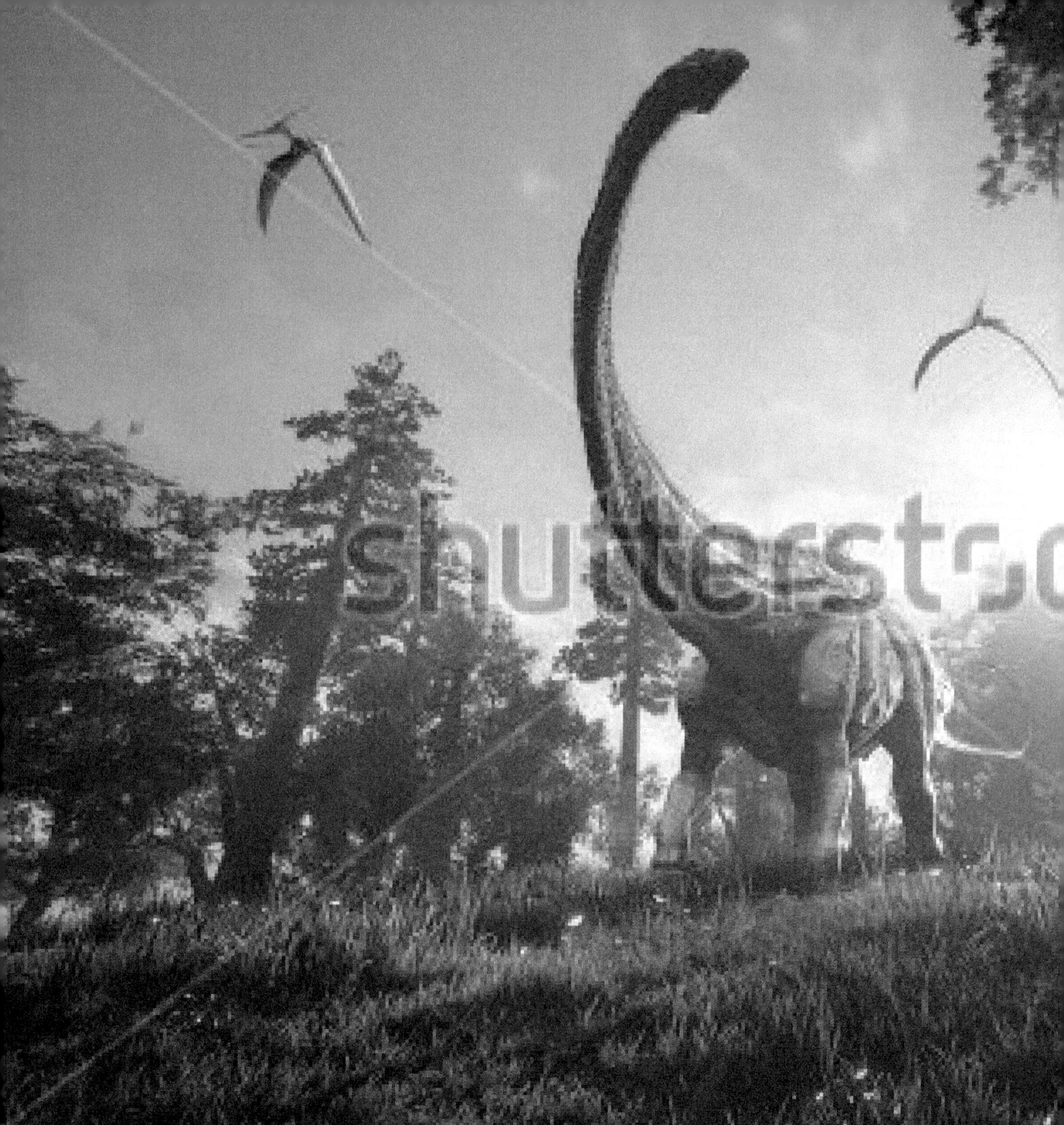

He called it Apatosaurus which meant "deceptive lizard".

But he also discovered somewhat larger set of bones.

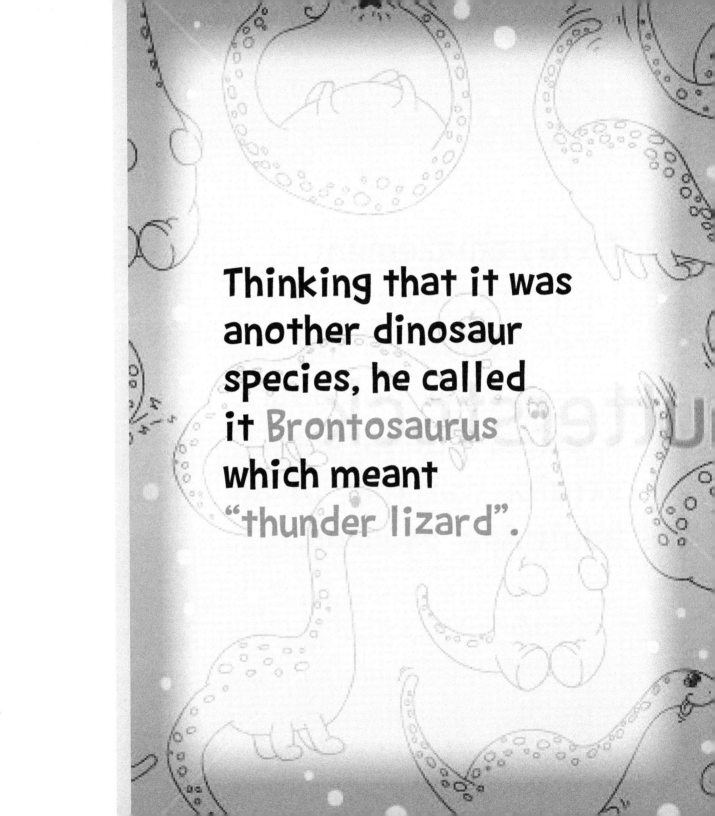

Thinking that it was another dinosaur species, he called it Brontosaurus which meant "thunder lizard".

To his amazement that the two set of large bones belong to the same dinosaur species. The larger version was that of an adult Apatosaurus.

What about its diet? What do you think they ate?

Apatosaurus are herbivores. Yes, they eat plants. They have to eat a lot of plants to support its very large size.

It ate all types of plants like ferns and trees. It swallowed directly its food and didn't chew it.

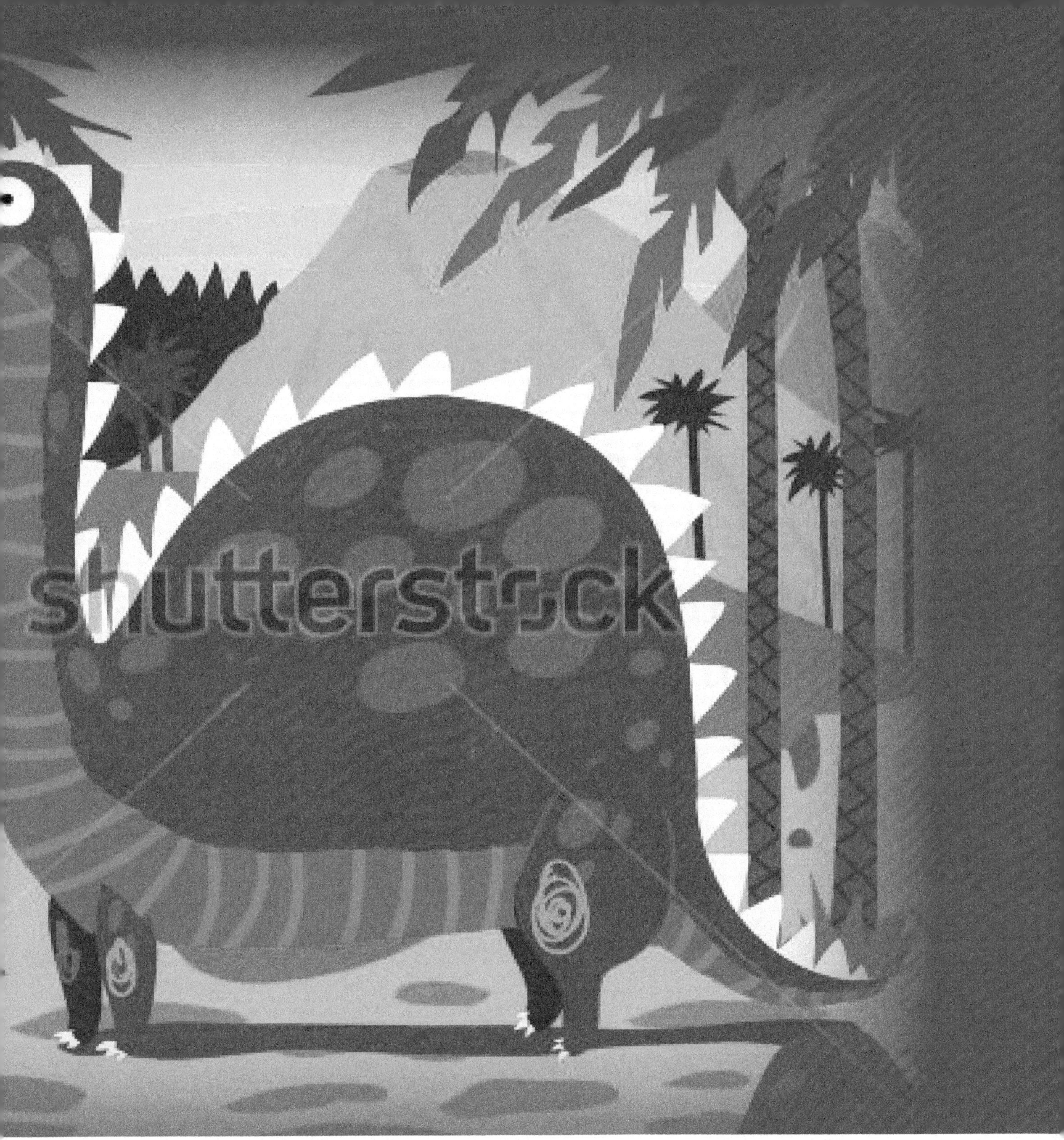

The digestion of the food was easily done through the gastroliths or stones found in its stomach.

Apatosaurus, just like the T-Rex, also became well known in social media. It is among the Transformer toy lines.

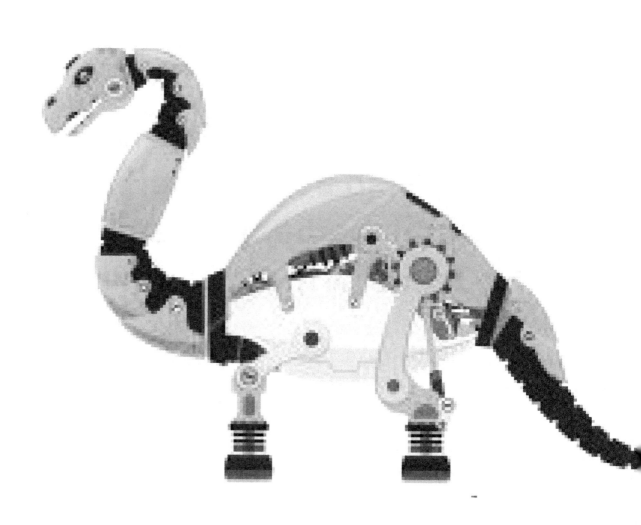

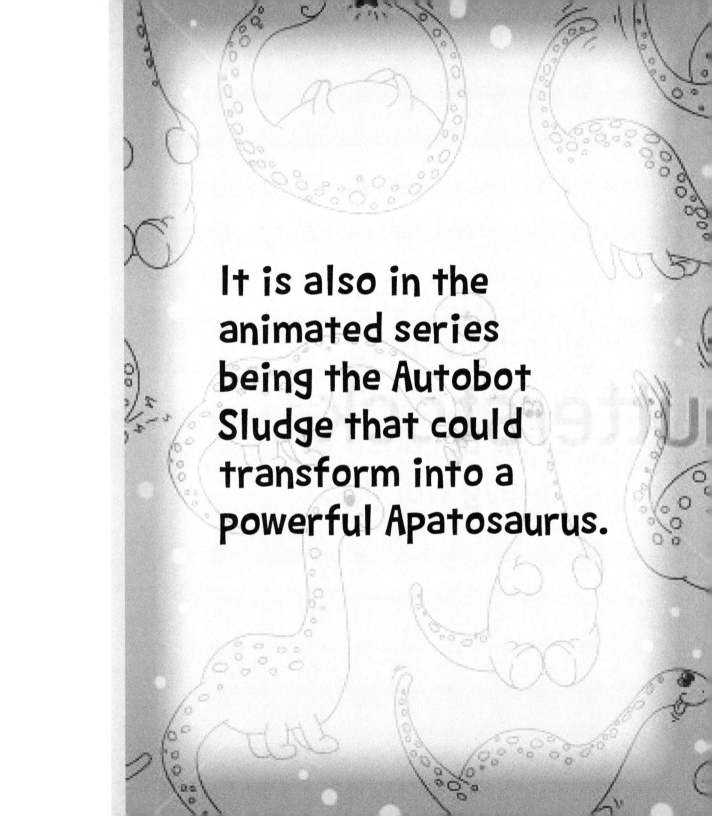

It is also in the animated series being the Autobot Sludge that could transform into a powerful Apatosaurus.

The Apatosaurus walked on their four legs. It moved so slow because of its heavy weight.

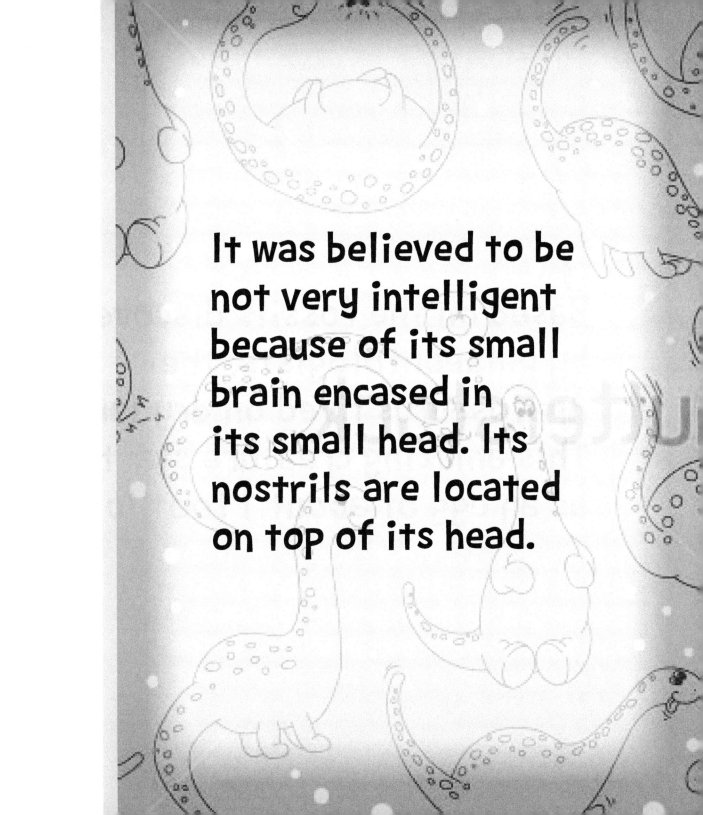

It was believed to be not very intelligent because of its small brain encased in its small head. Its nostrils are located on top of its head.

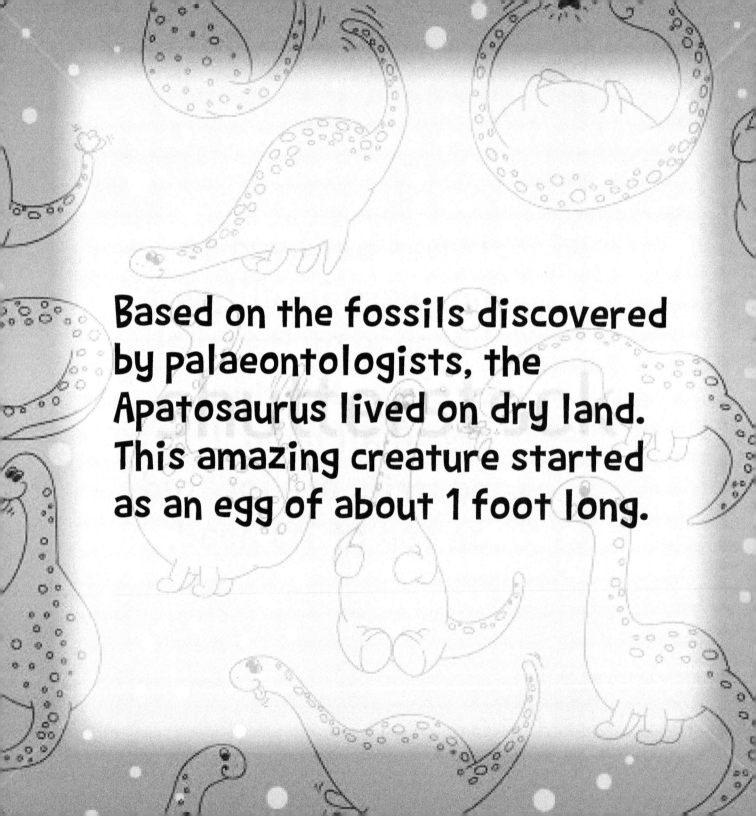

Based on the fossils discovered by palaeontologists, the Apatosaurus lived on dry land. This amazing creature started as an egg of about 1 foot long.

How do they distribute blood up to its very long neck and to their small heads?

Well, that's easily achieved by having a powerful heart and high blood pressure.

It made big noise by whipping its tail to scare intruders.

These are thundering facts that one should read and take note.

Why? Because they can't be with us anymore, not a chance, not a clue, we should just read and be amazed with the terrifying giant dinosaurs.

CPSIA information can be obtained
at www.ICGtesting.com
Printed in the USA
BVOW07s0127241017
498490BV00003B/4/P

9 781683 239833